BUILDING WEALTH IN THE TSP

YOUR ROAD MAP TO FINANCIAL FREEDOM AS A FERS EMPLOYEE

TABLE OF CONTENTS

Disclaimer:

This publication is designed to provide accurate and authoritative information in regard to the subject matter covered and has been compiled in good faith by the author. However, readers should be aware that this information may be incomplete, may contain errors or may have become out of date.

INTRODUCTION

> "If knowledge was the answer, we'd all be
> billionaires with six pack abs"
> **Derek Sivers**

You should be thanking yourself right now. Because not only do you have access to the TSP (The Thrift Savings Plan, one of the best retirement plans in the world!) but you then chose to pick up this book and educate yourself on how to get the most out of it. These two actions alone put you in an elite group.

But you are not out of the woods yet. After you finish this book, you will know a lot more about building wealth with the TSP. But I promise you that this book will not make you wealthy or financially free. The only thing that does that is action. Real, practical, and thought-out action.

The principals in this book can give you direction but it is up to you to decide how well they will work for you. And that takes effort. But because you have already chosen to read this book, I am confident that you have what it takes to build wealth and create an incredible life.

I am not just talking about money. There is much more in life than your TSP balance and it is up to you to make it happen.

Note: *This book is not meant to be a full textbook with every detail about your TSP. There are many sources online, including the OPM website, that include that sort of detail. This book is intended to be a quick-start guide to getting the most out of your TSP regardless of where you are at in your career.*

CHAPTER 1:

WHAT MAKES THE TSP SO AWESOME

Before I show you how to get the very most out of the TSP, it is important to know why we like the TSP in the first place. After all, there are many different ways and accounts to save for retirement. Some of these include an IRA, Roth IRA, 401(k), savings account, or regular brokerage account. And while some of these accounts can be used along with your TSP account, I hope to show you the innate advantages that come from maximizing your TSP first.

And before we get too far, I want to make sure that readers know that this book is primarily meant for federal employees under FERS (Federal Employee Retirement System). Other groups that participate in the TSP (CSRS Federal Employees, Military Service Members) can get tremendous value from reading and applying the principles in this book, but just know that some details won't apply perfectly to other groups.

The Match

The match is one of the most well known aspects of the TSP, but I would be amiss if I didn't mention it for those who might not be as familiar with it.

Your agency offers a match that can add up to 5% of your salary as long as you contribute at least that much yourself. The 5% is broken down into the following parts:

The 1st 1%- Your agency will automatically contribute 1% of your salary into your TSP account regardless of how much you contribute (even if you don't contribute at all). But in most cases, you'll have to work with the government for at least 3 years to become vested* in this amount.

*Being vested means you can take that money with you even if you leave federal service.

The next 3%- Your agency will match dollar for dollar the first 3% of your pay that you choose to contribute.

The next 2%- Your agency will then match 50 cents of every dollar of the next 2% of your base pay that you contribute.

This chart illustrates how this works:

% of Salary That You Contribute	Your Agency's Contribution	Total % Contributed to Your TSP
0%	1%	1%
1%	2%	3%
2%	3%	5%
3%	4%	7%
4%	4.5%	8.5%
5%	5%	10%
More than 5%	5%	Your Contribution + 5%

To summarize, if federal employees don't want to leave any money on the table then it generally makes sense to contribute at least 5% of your salary into your TSP account every pay period.

And often, it makes sense to invest much more than 5% but you have to start somewhere.

The Funds

When talking with federal employees about their TSP and the different funds (G, F, C, S, I, and L funds), I have noticed that there tends to be 3 different competency levels.

Level 1: This group gets most of their information from their coworkers as well as from some research online. They know enough to invest their TSP but they don't really understand what their choices mean. Most of the people I talk with fall into this category.

Level 2: This group has done a substantial amount of research and is starting to feel competent with investing. They learn about all the different investment options that exist outside the TSP and they wish that the TSP had more options.

Level 3: This group has done a lot of research on their own and has realized that in investing, sometimes less is more. They know what options exist outside the TSP but they also know how great the TSP funds are.

But here is the most important question: Which group has the best retirement outcomes? In my experience, level 3. Obviously there are exceptions, but this is what I have seen. This group knows enough to make very educated investment decisions but they keep it simple and they invest consistently.

This group understands that despite there being thousands of funds on the private side, they aren't necessarily better than what the TSP has. The TSP funds are simple, straightforward, and easy to understand as investments go. And these attributes make them ideal for the millions of employees who use the TSP.

But don't let the simplicity make you believe that they don't perform as well as more complicated outside investments. Most of the time, TSP participants do just as well if not much better than people who are invested elsewhere. And the next section goes over why this is.

The Fees

It costs money to run and manage the TSP funds and these costs are covered by the people that invest in the different funds. Whether you know it or not, you pay a portion of your TSP balance every year to cover the TSP's costs. The good news is that the fees are right around .042% (in 2019) of your account balance.

That means it costs about 42 cents per $1,000 you have in the TSP per year.

For example, if your TSP balance is $100,000, then you'll pay right around $42 per year.

Now, you may be bummed that you have to pay anything at all but you may not feel as bad if you compare the TSP to the average 401(k). Some studies have shown that 401(k) fees vary widely between 0.2% and 5% with the average right around 1%[1]. Other studies have even shown the average 401(k) fees to be closer to 2% but for this next example let's be conservative and use 1%.

To put this in perspective, when you are paying $42 per year on your $100,000 TSP balance, your 401(k) counterpart is paying $1,000!

This type of difference becomes even more dramatic over an entire career.

Let's do a quick example. Say one person invested $500 a month in funds that earned 8% per year. He kept investing for 40 years. At retirement, he'd have more than 1.6 million dollars. But if he would have paid a 1% fee every year, he would have only ended up with about 1.2 million dollars. That is a difference of $400,000 over a career!

But just to clarify my position, I am not opposed to fees in general. If a product or service is worth the fee that you are paying then by all means continue paying it. But if a higher fee is not accompanied with a higher value then it may be worth making a change.

Now, as you can probably tell, I really like the TSP. I am not saying that it is perfect but in general, it does a really good job at building wealth. And my goal for the rest of the book is to show you how to do just that.

[1]**https://smartasset.com/retirement/what-are-401k-fees#:~:text=The%20cost%20is%20even%20greater,between%200.2%25%20and%205%25.**

CHAPTER 2:

THE POTENTIAL OF YOUR TSP

Depending on where you are at in your career, you may or may not have seen what happens when patience, consistency, and discipline collide in the TSP. If you don't know already, the results are spectacular. The results are normal people who are incredibly well prepared for a retirement that they never thought possible. This is especially true when we combine the power of the TSP with all your other benefits (I'll touch on these benefits at the end of the book).

But on the other side of the coin, we all have heard the common regret of "I wish I would have started investing earlier". Or "If only I knew then what I know now". But unfortunately, there is nothing we can do to change the past. Fortunately, we can learn from our own past as well as the past of others to make our future bright despite our mistakes.

Because we all hear the regretful almost-retiree talking about starting earlier, I figured it could be helpful for all of us to see an example of why investing early and consistently makes such a difference. Or in other words, why it pays to be the tortoise (patient, consistent, and disciplined) instead of the hare in the race of an incredible retirement and a robust TSP.

In this example, our tortoise fed is named Julie and our hare fed is named Robert. They both start their careers at age 27 and both make $75,000/year. We'll assume that their salary stays the same for their entire career to keep the numbers easy. Julie, right out of the gate, decides to invest 10% of her salary into the TSP. She got used to living on the lower amount and never thought much about it. Robert, on the other hand, decides that he is very far from retirement and will opt out of the TSP for now.

Now let's fast forward 10 years. Both Julie and Robert are 37 and they both think about their TSP again. Julie realizes that she has already accumulated $169,781 (we'll assume a 8% return for this entire example) and is pleasantly surprised. Robert talks to Julie and realizes that he really needs to start using his TSP. He decides to take a pretty drastic cut to his lifestyle to start contributing 10% of his salary into the TSP as well.

Fast forward 10 years again. They are both 47 and Julie now has $536,325 in her TSP and Robert has $169,781. They talk again and Robert gets fiercely competitive. He wants to contribute more than Julie so he takes another drastic cut to his lifestyle and starts contributing 20% of his salary into his TSP. Julie decides to stick to her 10%.

Fast forward 10 years one last time. They are both 57 and Julie is ready to retire. She has accumulated a whopping $1,327,666 in her TSP. She has plenty to cover the gap between now and when she starts drawing social security as well as for the years after. She is confident in her retirement and her financial freedom. She buys a vacation home and lives a retirement that she didn't think was possible.

Robert has done pretty well too. He has accumulated $649,643 in his TSP but decides to work a few extra years because he doesn't want to eat through a major portion of his TSP trying to fill the gap before he starts social security. He too has a good retirement but definitely doesn't have the same cushion and freedom that Julie now enjoys.

In the end, Julie ended up with more than twice the amount of retirement savings than Robert but this is not very surprising by itself. The surprising part shows up when we look at how much they each put into the TSP themselves. This charts makes it a little easier to see:

Note: This example ignores inflation, pay raises, and agency contributions.

Contributions

	Julie	Robert
1st Decade	$ 75,000.00	$ -
2nd Decade	$ 75,000.00	$ 75,000.00
3rd Decade	$ 75,000.00	$150,000.00
Total	$225,000.00	$225,000.00

Both Julie and Robert contributed the same amount to their TSP accounts during their careers but **when** they contributed made all the difference in the world. Julie was consistent the whole time while Robert had a late start and rushed to catch up near the end.

And while the details and amounts are different, I have seen this same story play out over and over again in real life. There are those feds who start early and stay consistent and are pleasantly surprised how much they end up with. And there are those who rush to catch up near the end. And as we have seen, the results tend to be dramatically different between the two groups.

Now, I don't write this to discourage those who might have had a late start. We all have things we wish we could go back and change. But, all we have is now and there is still so much we can do to prepare for the future.

If you want help knowing what you need to do to be best prepared for retirement, it may make sense to talk to a financial professional who understands your needs and federal benefits. But regardless of where we are at or what we have already done, we can all do something today to make your future that much brighter.

Chapter Summary: Regardless of what you have done in the past or where you are at in the career. Do what you have to **NOW** to get the most out of your benefits and retirement.

CHAPTER 3:

DO I HAVE ENOUGH?

A t this point, I hope you are feeling motivated and ready to take action. You should now understand how powerful of a tool the TSP can be, and if you are like many of the feds that I talk to, their next question is "How much should I be putting in my TSP to be ready for retirement"? Or for those closer to retirement, the question is "Do I have enough in my TSP to retire"?

I get these questions all the time and understandably so. Everyone wants to know where they stand, but interestingly enough I hear the same concern from those with 100k in their TSP as well as from those with 2 million. And what makes it so difficult is that for some 100k is enough but for others, 2 million may not be enough to make it through retirement.

What makes this question so hard is that everyone's retirement plans, goals, and needs are different. Some people have no consumer debt, no mortgage, and all their expenses are covered by their pension and social security. They really don't need much if any from their TSP in retirement other than fun money. Others may still be paying off their mortgage or may have higher lifestyle goals in retirement. Everyone has a different idea for what an ideal retirement looks like but the tricky part is knowing if your finances can support your choices.

The 4% Rule

Many people have been using the 4% rule to give them a place to start when planning for retirement. For those who haven't heard about this rule, it basically says that you can conservatively withdraw 4% of your initial retirement savings every year and not have to worry about running out of money. So for someone retiring with $400,000, 4% would be $16,000/year or about $1,333 per month.

That being said, not everyone can afford to only withdraw 4% of their TSP every year. The good news is that the 4% rule is conservative and many people can withdraw more and still not run out of money.

For example, a popular investment allocation for retirees (note: popularity doesn't mean it is the best option for **you**) is to invest in 60% stocks and 40% bonds. Or in TSP language, 60% in C,S, and I funds and 40% in the F and G funds. And the long-term return of this allocation is between 7%-8%. So technically, if you earned 7% every year, you could withdraw that same amount without touching your principle.

For example, let's say you retire with $400,000 in your TSP and you earn 7% per year. That means that if you withdraw $28,000 (7% of $400,000) every year, you'd still have your initial $400,000 at the end of retirement.

The problem though is that real life is never that simple. A 60/40 (60% stocks and 40% bonds) portfolio may have an average return of 7%-8% but one year may be 2% and the next year 14%. If someone was to withdraw 7% in a year that only made 2%, they would then be tapping into some of their original investment which then would not be around to grow the following year. Over time, this could seriously deplete your retirement savings depending on what the market does in years to come.

As you can see, this is why it becomes so difficult to answer the question of "do I have enough?" Because often, it simply depends. It depends on your needs, the market, interest rates, tax rates, and much more.

This is why the 4% rule has become popular. It is simple and conservative. And this is the type of strategy that makes sense for most feds. Now, I don't mean that everyone should use the 4% rule specifically. I simply mean that everyone needs to find a strategy that makes sense for them and at the same time is simple, conservative, with a good margin of error. This way you will be prepared to adjust as changes and curveballs come your way.

One big potential curveball that might affect all of us is the depletion of social security. It is well known that at the current rate, there won't be enough funds to pay out full benefits starting in 2035[2]. Now, the government will probably come up with a way to fill the gap but it will have to come from somewhere and that somewhere is usually us, the taxpayers. And regardless of what happens to social security, that is just the tip of the iceberg when it comes to the benefits federal retirees rely on from the federal government.

Now, I am not trying to say that you should plan on the government going under. First, the odds of that are very very small. And second, if the government does go under then we would have bigger problems to worry about.

All I am trying to say is that the TSP is one of your few benefits that you have control over. You control how much you invest, how you invest, and how you use it in retirement. And because you have control, the TSP is one of the best tools to fill all your retirement gaps. And like I mentioned, it is sometimes hard to know what your retirement gap will be with all the unknowns with future inflation rates, tax rates, social security, and more.

This is why when feds ask me how much they should be investing, I tell them "as much as you can". It is much easier to work with "too much" money at retirement than not enough. And odds are, things will go a lot better than the worst case scenario, and you will still have plenty.

That being said, I don't endorse postponing all types of trips, entertainment, and nice things till retirement just in the name of filling your TSP as much as possible. You have to find a balance that works for you now, but also takes care of your future needs as well.

And just like anything else, the sooner you start, the easier it is to be prepared. This is why it is so important to start planning as early as possible in your career so that you can make all the necessary adjustments as you go. It is much more painful and difficult to make a measurable difference in the last 2 years before retirement. If you haven't already, start now and you will thank yourself over and over again.

[2]**https://www.ssa.gov/policy/docs/ssb/v70n3/v70n3p111.html**

CHAPTER 4:

DO YOU REALLY UNDERSTAND WHAT YOUR LIFE SAVINGS IS INVESTED IN?

The TSP (Thrift Savings Plan) is the largest employer sponsored savings plan in the world and it (or at least should) plays a huge role in the retirement of every FERS federal employee.

Thousands of millionaires are made every year just from effectively using their TSP account.

But honestly, unless someone has at least a basic knowledge of the TSP Funds then it is very difficult to be successful in the TSP long term

The Essentials

There are only 5 core fund options in the TSP. Here they are with a brief explanation of what they invest in.

G Fund: Invests in U.S. Treasury Bonds. .

F Fund: Invests in various types of U.S.-based bonds.

C Fund: Invests in 500 of some of the largest U.S. companies (Tracks the S&P 500).

S Fund: Invests in most other major U.S. companies excluding the S&P 500.

I Fund: Invests in the major companies in Europe, Australasia, and the Far East.

Note: There are also L funds in the TSP but these funds are just a mixture of the core 5 funds. I'll discuss the L funds more below.

To keep things simple I am going to break the TSP funds into 2 categories. Aggressive and conservative.

The Conservative Funds

The G and F funds are the more conservative of the 5 funds because they don't have the tendency to be as volatile as the others. But as a price for being more stable, they don't have the potential to grow like the other funds do.

The G fund actually guarantees that any money invested in it won't lose value but it has only averaged about a 2% annual return over the last 10 years.

The F fund can drop in value but is still very stable compared to the other funds. It has averaged about 3.6% annual return over the last 10 years.

Here is a chart showing the return of these 2 funds over different periods as of 8-11-21:

	G Fund Government Securities Investment Fund	**F Fund** Fixed Income Index Investment Fund
Objective	Ensure preservation of capital and generate returns above those of short-term U.S. Treasury securities.	Match the performance of the Bloomberg Barclays U.S. Aggregate Bond Index.
Return Year-to-date	0.77%	-0.37%
☑ 1 year	1.09%	-0.52%
☑ 3 year	1.75%	5.79%
☑ 5 year	1.99%	3.25%
☑ 10 year	1.95%	3.58%
☑ Lifetime	4.76%	6.06%
Inception date	4/1/1987	1/29/1988
Risk	●●●●● Low	●●●●● Low-medium

As you can see, the F fund has decreased slightly in value over the last year primarily because of low interest rates.

The Problem With The G and F Funds

As many people approach retirement they often will put the majority of their TSP accounts into a combination of the G and F funds. And while putting a portion of your money in conservative funds can be a very strategic thing, many people take this way too far.

The G and F funds probably won't lose value but they probably won't grow much either. Overtime, this lack of major growth as well as inflation can take a huge toll on your money.

For instance, if the prices of things go up every year (inflation) and your investments aren't growing enough to more than make up for it, then you may deplete your TSP much faster than you had planned.

Now I am not saying that the G and F funds aren't good funds. They are great funds and they do exactly what they are designed to do. But with that being said, you will want to make sure you also have investments that will help you maintain your standard of living over the course of your entire retirement.

The Aggressive Funds

The C, S, and I funds are the more aggressive of the funds in the TSP.

The reason they are called "aggressive" is because they have a much higher chance of sustaining major growth over time. But because of this, they can also be much more volatile than the G and F funds.

For example, the C fund lost more than 35% in 2008 but regained it all and more in the next couple of years.

You shouldn't invest any money into these funds that you are going to need in the next few years. These funds will perform better in the long term but are not as predictable in the short-term.

Here is a chart showing the return of these 3 funds over different periods as of 8-11-21:

	C Fund Common Stock Index Investment Fund	S Fund Small cap stock Index investment fund	I Fund International Stock Index Investment Fund
Objective	Match the performance of the Standard and Poor's 500 (S&P 500) Index.	Match the performance of the Dow Jones U.S. Completion Total Stock Market Index.	Match the performance of the MSCI EAFE (Europe, Australasia, Far East) Index.
Return Year-to-date	17.98%	14.04%	9.77%
☑ 1 year	36.42%	51.07%	30.49%
☑ 3 year	18.11%	17.40%	7.99%
☑ 5 year	17.32%	17.27%	9.70%
☑ 10 year	15.37%	14.39%	6.48%
☑ Lifetime	11.23%	10.65%	5.49%
Inception date	1/29/1988	5/1/2001	5/1/2001
Risk	●●●●● Medium	●●●●● Medium-high	●●●●● High

The L Funds

The most important thing to understand about the L funds is that they are not independent funds. They are simply different combinations of the core 5 funds that we have been talking about.

What makes them different however is that each L fund is designed to automatically become more conservative over time. So in theory, one could invest in a L fund and never have to change their investment allocation for the rest of their career.

CHAPTER 5:

TSP INVESTMENT STRATEGIES DURING YOUR CAREER

Back in March of 2020, I spoke to a federal employee who was pretty proud of himself. He had decided to move his entire TSP balance into the G fund just a couple months before the coronavirus shook the stock market. By the time I spoke with him, the market had dropped more than 30%.

He had a TSP balance of about $280,000 so a 30% drop would have brought his balance down to $196,000 (assuming he was invested 100% in the C fund). Now, I am not sure what funds he was investing in but the bottom line is that he would have "lost" a lot of money. But since he had everything in the G fund when the drop happened, his balance was safe and sound.

Some would say that this guy just saved 80k. But I would say that this guy will probably lose a few 100k in the process. Let me tell you why.

The problem with selling right before a "down market" is two fold. First, it is very difficult to predict a down market. Second, now that you moved everything into the G fund (even if we assume that you correctly predicted a down market), when do you move it back? The only thing harder than knowing when the market will go down is knowing when it will recover.

Even professional investors have not been able to predict the market consistently. Anyone can get lucky once and a while but doing it consistently is a different story.

Warren Buffet, one of the most successful investors of all time, once said "we've long felt that the only value of stock forecasters is to make fortune tellers look good". So even Warren Buffet, who has made billions in investing, does not try to time the market.

With all that being said, I actually think it is a great thing that this fed saved 80k. Because technically, if someone could successfully time the market, they would do much better than any other strategy. All I am worried about is what he is going to do now and in the future. How much money and sleep will he lose trying to decide exactly when to make his next move. At least to me, this seems like a big gamble to make with your retirement savings.

Now, I am not always opposed to risk. When we are talking about investing, risk is always a part of the equation. The trick is to limit and manage your risk to give your savings room to grow while protecting your downside as best you can.

The good news is that as FERS federal employees, you have a leg up on most others. You enjoy both social security, a pension, FEHB (your health insurance), and other great retirement benefits. For many feds, these benefits will provide a great base for their retirement lifestyle with their TSP filling whatever gap is left. And the trick is to try to optimize your TSP allocation to be able to fill that gap for the rest of your life.

When you are young and early in your career, it often makes sense to put the majority of your TSP in the C, S, and I funds. And because young feds tend to have a lot of time before retirement, they don't mind that these funds bounce around because overtime, they grow at a fast rate. But as you progress through your career and approach retirement, it often makes sense to introduce more of the F and G fund. These funds won't grow nearly as fast, but they will provide more of the stability you need in retirement. But even in retirement, I almost never recommend going 100% into the G fund. The G fund is safe but won't grow enough to beat inflation and maintain your lifestyle over time.

Having a good mixture of funds allows the more stable funds (G and F) to provide consistent cash for your retirement lifestyle and the other funds (C, S, and I) to beat inflation and continue to grow your wealth.

At this point, some of you might have noticed that I haven't mentioned the L funds. And this is because the L funds are not independent funds. They are just a mixture of the other 5 funds.

For example, this is the allocation of the L 2030 fund as of July 2020:

July 2020

■ G Fund 32.95%

■ F Fund 6.93%

■ C Fund 30.54%

■ S Fund 8.54%

■ I Fund 21.04%

Source: **https://www.tsp.gov/funds-lifecycle/l-2030/**

What makes the L funds useful is that the allocation will automatically become more conservative (transfer more to the F and G funds) as time goes on. The purpose of these funds are so that employees can "set it and forget it". In practice, feds pick the L fund that is closest to their retirement date and they don't have to think about it again.

My problem with the L funds is that this approach doesn't make sense for everyone. For example, I have a client who is close to retirement. Once he retires, his social security and pension income will be more than enough to pay for his expenses so he is not planning on using his TSP balance for some time.

In his case, we are able to invest his TSP more aggressively because he has a substantial amount of time before he needs the money. If he had chosen an L fund, the allocation would have been far too conservative for him.

The L funds are not bad funds but you have to make sure it makes sense for you before investing in them.

Always keep in mind that there is no perfect TSP allocation. It all depends on your situation and goals. The exact percentage of each fund that makes sense for you will often be different than what makes sense for your co-workers. The best thing to do is to educate yourself enough to make an informed decision. A financial advisor who understands the TSP can be a huge asset in this process as well. Because regardless of where you are in your career, getting your TSP right can make a huge difference over your career and retirement.

Once you come up with a TSP allocation plan that makes sense for you, stick to your plan. Don't worry about what the market is doing. Focus on what you can control and not on what you can't. You can't control the markets but you can control how much you set aside for retirement. You can't control the economy but you can control how well you plan for the future.

The good news is that by reading this book and educating yourself, you are taking one more step towards being prepared for whatever comes your way.

CHAPTER 6:

TSP LOANS/GETTING MONEY OUT

I have mixed feelings about TSP loans. For some they can be a saving grace in a bind but they are often misused. We all know that unexpected things happen in life and ideally none of us would ever have to touch our retirement savings to cover these emergencies.

But because life is often not ideal, there are certain times that a TSP loan might just be the best option even with the negative consequences.

One Last Check

Before truly considering a TSP loan, make sure to do one last check that you don't have any other funds that you can use.

The TSP should be one of the very last places to go for money.

When money is taken out of the TSP it can no longer grow and compound over time which can severely lower what your TSP balance could be at retirement. Also, if a TSP loan is not fully paid back by the time you leave government service then it will be counted as a taxable distribution.

So you may not want to take a TSP loan if you are leaving government service in the near future.

Getting Money Out While Your Still Working

There are 2 main ways of getting money out of your TSP while you are still working.

A loan or an in-service withdrawal.

The downside of an in-service withdrawal is that it can be subject to taxes as well as a 10% penalty if you are under age 59 and ½. But of course you won't need to pay the withdrawal back.

A TSP loan is often the better option because you won't owe taxes or a penalty and you will get the money back into your account once you pay it back.

This chart shows a comparison between an in-service withdrawal and a TSP loan

	In-Service Withdrawal	TSP Loan
Cost	Your retirement savings will be permanently lower because of this withdrawal	$50 Loan Fee
Effect on Taxes	Can be subject to taxes and a 10% early withdrawal penalty if under 59 and 1/2	None (unless you leave service before it is paid back)

The True Cost of a TSP Loan

But remember, the true cost of a TSP loan is not the $50 loan fee. It is the fact that the money that you take out of your TSP is not invested and can't grow during that time.

This can make a significant difference over time.

Paying Off High-Interest Debt

The first situation that it may make sense to use a TSP loan is to pay off high-interest loans such as credit cards.

In many cases, credit card interest can be 15%-20% while the current interest rate on a TSP loan is 1.375% (as of 3/30/21). Not to mention that any interest that you do pay on a TSP loan just goes back into your account.

But like always, we will want to make sure that we are solving the underlying problem and not just fighting symptoms. If our spending habits keep putting us into credit card debt then pulling from your TSP will only be a short-term fix.

I would only consider using the TSP for debt when you are fully committed to not accumulating more credit card debt.

Medical Emergency With HDHP

A high deductible health plan or HDHP can be a great way to save money in premiums but as the name suggests the deductibles are high.

This means that some people may be caught without the savings to cover the deductible when a medical event happens in their family.

The best way to pay the deductible in a high deductible plan is with an HSA or health savings account because of its great tax advantages. But for those that don't have an HSA and don't have the savings, a TSP loan may be the next best option so that they can preserve their credit.

Bad Credit

Emergencies often occur when we least expect them and some people may be caught financially unprepared. This can be even more stressful if bad credit prevents you from getting a loan at a reasonable rate.

In these situations, it can sometimes make sense to access the TSP to avoid more high-interest debt.

But as always, we should always do whatever we can to not put ourselves in this position in the first place.

For those with good credit, a HELOC (home equity line of credit) may be a better alternative to a TSP loan.

Another Reminder

As a general rule, I don't recommend a TSP loan unless it is really needed but in some circumstances it can be a great tool to provide flexibility in tough times.

BONUS CHAPTER:

TSP VS. IRA

B oth the TSP and IRAs have two different parts. The traditional side and the Roth side.

And in this book we are going to compare and contrast the traditional and Roth TSP to its IRA counterparts so that you have a better understanding of what makes sense for you.

Traditional TSP vs. Traditional IRA

The first thing to compare is the traditional TSP to a traditional IRA.

Both of these accounts are pre-tax accounts which means that you don't pay taxes when you put money in but you do when you take money out in retirement.

As a simplified example, let's say that you had $50,000 of taxable income from your job last year. If you would have invested $5,000 into either the traditional TSP or a traditional IRA, your taxable income would have been only $45,000. You are essentially deferring the taxes on that income until a later time.

But let's say that the $5,000 that you invested into either account grew to $20,000 over the next 20 years. When you withdraw the $20,000 in retirement the entire amount will be subject to taxes and not just the initial $5,000 that you invested.

The Match

One major difference between these two accounts is that as federal employees, your agency offers matching contributions if you invest in the TSP. Basically, your agency will contribute money into your TSP account based on how much you are contributing. There is no match when you invest in an IRA.

Contribution Limits

Another big difference between the TSP and IRAs is how much you can contribute every year.

As of 2021, you can invest significantly more into the TSP compared to IRAs. This chart shows the contribution limits for 2021.

2021 TSP and IRA Contribution Limits

	Normal Limits	If Age 50 or Older
TSP	$19,500	$26,000
IRA	$6,000	$7,000

HAWS FEDERAL ADVISORS

Am I Allowed to Contribute to Both a Traditional IRA and the Traditional TSP?

The short answer is yes you can. The long answer is that once your income surpasses certain limits then you won't be able to deduct your IRA contributions if you or your spouse is also enrolled in an employer sponsored plan (ie. the TSP).

This next section goes through this in detail.

Traditional IRA Contribution Deduction Income limits

When you contribute to the traditional TSP or a traditional IRA you are generally able to deduct these contributions on your taxes. This is always true for your TSP contributions.

However, once your income surpasses certain limits you may not be able to deduct your IRA contributions.

The rules will be different depending on which of the 2 categories you fall into.

1. **No Retirement Plan at Work:** If neither you and your spouse is covered under a retirement plan (ie. the TSP, 401k, 403b) then your traditional IRA contributions will always be tax deductible no matter your level of income.

2. **Retirement Plan at Work:** If at least one spouse is covered by a retirement plan at work then there are income thresholds for IRA deductions.

You can find the income thresholds on the IRS website or at this link:

https://www.irs.gov/retirement-plans/2021-ira-deduction-limits-effect-of-modified-agi-on-deduction-if-you-are-covered-by-a-retirement-plan-at-work

Traditional TSP and Traditional IRA Withdrawal Rules

Another big difference between the traditional TSP and traditional IRA is when/how you can take money out in retirement.

For most retirement accounts, there is a 10% penalty if you take out your money before age 59 and ½. The distribution may be subject to taxes as well.

However, if you retire from federal service after age 55 you are able to access your traditional TSP without this 10% penalty. If you are under the FERS special provisions then this will be age 50. And like always, money taken out of your traditional TSP will be subject to taxes.

What is important to know is that traditional IRAs don't waive this 10% penalty for those that retire after age 55 (or 50 for special provisions). IRA owners still have to wait until 59 and ½.

So if you are retiring in your fifties but before age 59 and ½ then there is often an advantage to keeping your money in the TSP and not rolling it into an IRA (until at least 59 and ½).

TSP Investment Fees Vs. IRA Investment Fees

Investment funds such as the C,S, I, F, and G funds cost money to run and the TSP covers these costs through charging fees. The good news is that the TSP fees are very low at about 0.04% depending on the fund.

This means that for every $1,000 that you have in the TSP, you pay 40 cents every year in investment fees.

But if we look at the funds on the private side (outside the TSP), we find the investment fees can easily be between 0.5%-2% to invest in an index fund or mutual fund. In the extremes, this means that you could be paying up to 50x to invest in certain funds compared to the TSP funds.

But as a financial planner myself who often charges fees, I am certainly not opposed to fees in general. Some things are 100% worth paying for.

The question that we all have to ask ourselves when buying anything (including investments) is if the product or service that I am receiving is worth the fees that I am paying. And unfortunately, the extra fees that we pay for expensive investment funds are often not worth it at all.

Many studies have shown that passive index-style investment funds, such as the funds in the TSP, often outperform those funds that have a more active strategy especially once we take the higher fees into account.

And the good news is that there are now many low-fee options on the private side as well. Vanguard and Fidelity have some great options to consider.

Can I Roll My Traditional IRA Into My Traditional TSP?

Yes, you are able to roll over a traditional IRA into your TSP during your career and even after you separate or retire from service.

Note: You can not roll a Roth IRA into your TSP even if you have a Roth TSP.

Roth TSP vs. Roth IRA

Now that we have compared the pre-tax (aka traditional) sides of the TSP and IRAs, now it is time to compare the Roth TSP and a Roth IRA.

They have a number of similarities and I get questions about both of them all the time. That being said, they have key differences that make a big difference in how the accounts can be used.

So let's get into the details...

The Similarities

Tax-Me-Now Accounts

This is often the most well known aspect of a Roth IRA or the Roth TSP. This means that you are only able to contribute after-tax money into these accounts. Unlike the traditional TSP or traditional IRA, you do not get a tax deduction for putting money into a Roth account.

But down the road in retirement (assuming you follow all the rules), you are then able to take money out of Roth accounts completely tax free. And one of the best parts is that you not only can access what you put in tax free, but you can also get all the money that your contributions had earned while in the account tax free.

For example, let's say you contribute $100,000 into the Roth TSP over your career and you invest it. At retirement time, your initial $100,000 contribution has grown to $200,000. You'd be able to access all $200,000 tax free.

Off Limits For 5 Years

Once you open a Roth IRA or start contributing to a Roth TSP, you have to wait at least 5 years to be able to access the earnings tax free.There are other withdrawal rules as well (like being at least 59 and ½) but this 5 year rule is often that one that gets forgotten.

For example, let's say you start a Roth IRA at age 60 while you are still working. You retire at age 62 and are excited to have some tax free money in retirement. Even though you are older than 59 and ½, you'd still have to wait 5 years from the time you opened the account to be able to access your earnings tax free.

The Differences

No RMDs (Required Minimum Distributions)

For those that are 72 and older, you have probably already dealt with RMDs. For those that haven't, RMDs require you to take a certain amount of money out of some types of retirement accounts starting at age 72. This is the government's way of not allowing you to take advantage of tax-advantaged accounts for your entire life.

If someone does not take a RMD (knowingly or unknowingly), they will have to pay a 50% penalty of whatever amount they didn't distribute. The government takes this very seriously.

The good news however, is that Roth IRAs are not subject to RMDs. This gives Roth IRA owners the flexibility to let their money grow tax free for as long as they'd like. They also enjoy the privilege of not worrying about if they have done their RMDs correctly or not.

Roth TSP owners are not so lucky. They, along with traditional TSP, traditional IRA, and 401(k) owners, are required to take RMDs starting at age 72.

Backdoor Roth IRA

Once your income is over certain limits, you are no longer able to contribute to a Roth IRA. There are no such limits for a Roth TSP. You can find these limits on the IRS website and they change over time.

But if you are a high-earner and would still like to get money into a Roth IRA there is a roundabout option. It is called a backdoor Roth IRA.

In a nutshell, a backdoor Roth strategy is used when you put money into a traditional IRA and then convert it into a Roth IRA. This works because while there are income limits to making direct contributions to a Roth IRA there are no income limits to converting money from a traditional IRA to a Roth IRA.

But as we mentioned earlier in this article, there are income limits for taking deductions for traditional IRA contributions. This means that once your income crosses certain limits you can still contribute to a traditional IRA but you won't be able to claim a tax deduction for doing so.

But you might ask, why would you want to contribute money to a traditional IRA if you don't get a tax deduction for doing so? Some people do so to then be able to use the backdoor Roth strategy.

Here is an example of how it could work.

Let's say you have a traditional IRA and a Roth IRA which both have a balance of $0. Unfortunately you make too much money to put money directly into a Roth IRA and you also make too much money to deduct your traditional IRA contributions.

Because of this you decide to put $6,000 (the max for 2021) into your traditional IRA knowing that you won't get a tax deduction for doing so. At that point you could then transfer that $6,000 into your Roth IRA and because that money was after-tax to begin with, you won't have to pay taxes on the conversion.

The result is that you were able to get money into a Roth IRA despite being over the income limits.

Note: If you had taken a tax deduction for the original traditional IRA contribution then you will have to pay taxes when you transfer money to a Roth IRA

Backdoor Roth IRA Example

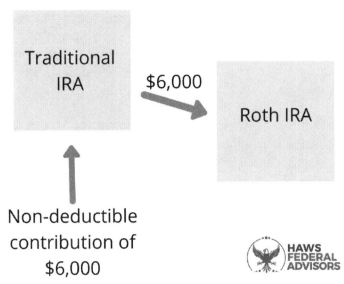

But there are certainly a number of things to watch out for.

The Pro-rata Rule

The pro-rata rule states that if you do a Roth conversion then the tax status of whatever you convert to a Roth IRA will be proportional to all the money you have in traditional IRAs.

For example, if you have $1,000 in your traditional IRA that is pre-tax and $1,000 that is post-tax then the IRS will assume that for every dollar that you convert over to a Roth IRA, half of it will be post-tax and half of it will be pre-tax. So if you decide to convert $1,000 from your traditional IRA to a Roth IRA then you will have to pay taxes on $500 of the conversion.

The pro-rata rule will still apply even if you have multiple IRAs.

For example, if you have one traditional IRA with $500 of pre-tax money and a second traditional IRA with $500 of post-tax money then regardless of which IRA you convert to a Roth IRA the IRS will count half of the conversion as taxable because that is the proportion across all your IRAs.

However, one way to potentially get around this is by moving all your pre-tax traditional IRA money into your traditional TSP. This would then allow you to convert any amount of post-tax money into a Roth IRA without tax consequences.

The Five-year Rule

Whenever you do a Roth conversion it starts a 5-year clock. If you distribute the conversion principle within the 5 years then it may be subject to a penalty if you are still younger than age 59 and ½.

Note: As of September 2021, the next tax plan is considering getting rid of the ability to do backdoor Roth IRA contributions. See the IRA website for the latest information.

CHAPTER 7:

WHAT TO DO WITH YOUR TSP AT RETIREMENT

The TSP has served you well over a long career but now it is time to retire. My retiring clients often ask things like "Is the TSP still the best option in this new stage of life? Some people talk about moving it to an IRA, but all I've known is the TSP. I've done well enough investing my TSP during my career but I really don't know how I should invest in my retirement."

Unfortunately, there is no black and white answer. There is not one single solution that fits the needs of every single federal employee out there. Everyone, (that means you too) needs to educate themselves enough to know the basic pros and cons of this decision because it can make a big difference over a long retirement.

IRA?

An IRA is a great tool and is widely used by those working in the private sector. It is less common among feds however, because they have access to the TSP.

The main advantages of an IRA in retirement is the flexibility. You have much more wiggle room with withdrawal options, as well as investment options. The one potential problem that comes with more choices is the complexity. The TSP's strength lies in the fact that it is so simple and easy to use. There are limited investment options, but they meet the needs of most feds just fine. If you want to have more flexibility to withdraw and invest funds in more complex ways and you don't mind paying a little more to invest in private sector funds then maybe an IRA is the right choice.

It is important to note that many financial advisors will tell you to roll your TSP into an IRA. This is not always a bad thing especially if you'd like your advisor to manage the account for you. Just remember that most advisors get paid to manage money. The more money they manage, the more money they make. Because advisors can't directly manage your TSP they will often advise you to simply roll it out into an IRA so that they can manage it.

Now, I am not saying that all financial advisors will throw your interests aside just to make more money. There are many advisors out there who truly put their clients before themselves. As an advisor myself, I have definitely seen both the good and bad in the industry.

My advice to you is to not be afraid to ask your advisor when you don't understand why he/she advises a certain way. An advisor that is worth their salt will be able to walk you through the reasons why a certain action makes the most sense for you in the long run.

The TSP Vs. IRA chapter in the book goes into more detail into the big differences between the TSP and an IRA.

Cons Of Keeping Your TSP

An IRA has one major advantage over the TSP. Flexibility. As long as you meet some basic criteria, you can withdraw money out of your IRA however you'd like. With the TSP however, there are a number of rules that control how and when you can take money out. Many people find it easier to control retirement income with an IRA over the TSP.

For example, when you distribute money from your TSP you can't choose which funds it comes out of. It will come out proportionally from the funds that you are invested in.

Let's say you have 50% of your money in the G fund and the other 50% in the C fund. If you take out $100 then $50 will come from the G fund and $50 from the C fund. This might be an issue if the market is down and you'd prefer not to sell the C fund until the market recovered.

How to Invest During Retirement

Investing during retirement is often crucial to ensure that your money lasts longer than you do. Not only are you trying to make your money last but you are also trying to beat inflation and maintain your standard of living. Assuming an inflation rate of 3%, it takes about 25 years for the value of your money to be cut in half. Many retirements these days last at least 25 years.

Now I can't say exactly what investment strategy is the best for you but I can give some general advice. The major difference in investing strategies between feds depends on how much of your TSP you need every year, your other income sources (social security, Federal Pension, ect), your timeline, and your goals.

A good way to approach retirement investing is to think about 3 different buckets. The first bucket is your cash bucket. This is the bucket that you will be drawing from to fund your living expenses. You will always want 3-5 years of living expenses (whatever isn't covered already from other income sources i.e. FERS Pension, social security) in your cash bucket so that you can wait out any down markets without having to sell your investments when they're low. This cash bucket gives you security and freedom.

The second bucket is your income bucket. This bucket will invest in bonds and other income producing investment that we can use to replenish your cash bucket over the years. There should be enough money in this bucket to cover the next 5-10 years after your cash bucket. This bucket won't grow as much as the 3rd bucket but it will be more steady.

The last bucket is your growth bucket. This bucket is where you invest in things that will have good growth over time. These investments will have up years and down years but over time they will provide the growth needed to beat inflation. This bucket will have all your money that you don't need for at least 10 years. You have your cash and income buckets so you don't have to touch your growth bucket in the years that these investments go down.

Deciding how much should be in each bucket is a mixture between an art and a science. You will have to see what makes sense for you and your retirement needs, but thinking about your retirement investments in this way can get you on the right path.

The Best TSP Withdrawal Options (And The Worst One)

The first thing for you to know is that there are only a number of ways that you can withdraw money from your TSP.

Note: These options are significantly better than they used to be since the TSP Modernization Act.

Here are the 3 main ways to withdraw money from your TSP:

TSP Withdrawal Options

- **Scheduled Installment Payments**
  - monthly, quarterly, or annual
  - fixed dollar amount or based on life expectancy
- **Single Withdrawals**
- **Annuity Purchases**

Note: The TSP only allows one withdrawal every 30 calendar days.

You are allowed to use any combination of these 3 withdrawal options and there is no limit to how many withdrawals you can make in retirement. However, the TSP does limit you to one withdrawal every 30 days.

But let's say that you set up a monthly installment payment to pay you $1,000 per month, you would still be able to take single withdrawals while also receiving installment payments as long as the single withdrawals are at least 30 days apart.

You are able to change the amount, frequency, and withdrawal source (traditional TSP or Roth) at any point for installment payments.

When making a single withdrawal the minimum withdrawal amount is $1,000. There is also a $25 monthly minimum for installment payments.

Should I Take a TSP Annuity?

With the annuity option you would give your TSP balance or at least a portion of it, to an annuity provider (Metlife has the current contract to provide these to federal retirees if desired). They would guarantee you a fixed income for a certain amount of time. You can also have the annuity produce a monthly payment for the rest of your life and the amount of your payment will be set based on your life expectancy.

The major downside of this option is the limited flexibility and reversibility. Once you make this decision, it is very difficult to get access to your money other than what they pay you every month. This option offers security but very limited flexibility.

Not to mention that federal employees tend to already have a large amount of fixed income with a pension and social security. And while fixed income is great to have, you will still want sufficient savings and investments to have the flexibility to deal with the uncertainties of life as they come up.

TSP Withdrawal Strategies

The majority of people have their retirement savings/investments in three different types of accounts. Traditional (pre-tax), Roth (after-tax), or taxable (non-retirement account/brokerage account).

I am going to focus on just traditional and Roth in this book because the TSP does not include taxable accounts.

And when/how you distribute money from each of these accounts will ultimately determine how much you pay in taxes over the course of your retirement.

Here is a basic rundown of how money is taxed when it comes out of these accounts.

Traditional

Your traditional TSP, traditional 401k, and traditional IRA would all fall into this category. These types of accounts are all pre-tax which means that you will have to pay taxes on anything you take out.

These distributions will be taxed as ordinary income which is the worst type of income to have for tax purposes. This means that they will be taxed at your marginal tax rate.

Roth

This includes your Roth TSP, Roth 401k, and Roth IRA. Since you already paid taxes when you put money into these accounts, it all comes out tax-free.

For obvious reasons, tax-free income is a great thing to have in retirement.

Which Should You Take Out First?

Now that we know how each type of retirement account is taxed, we have to ask ourselves what the best strategy might be to reduce taxes as much as possible across your retirement.

As a general rule, it can often make sense to use traditional money first in retirement. This way you allow your other investments (especially Roth) to continue to grow in a more tax efficient way.

Also, starting at age 72, all traditional investments will be subject to RMDs (required minimum distributions) which means you'll have to start withdrawing a portion of your account every year which will be subject to taxes. And if your traditional assets have a high balance at age 72 then these forced withdrawals might push you up to a higher tax bracket.

Note: One of the only retirement accounts that is **not** subject to RMDs is a Roth IRA. This is why many people opt to roll their Roth TSP (if they have one) to a Roth IRA in retirement.

The More Roth the Merrier

One strategy that we often use with our clients is doing mini Roth conversions in retirement.

A Roth conversion is done by moving money from a traditional account to a Roth account. Because you can't move money from the traditional TSP to the Roth TSP, this strategy will have to be done with a Roth IRA

We do this by looking at how much room they have before they hit the next tax bracket and we convert up to that amount.

For example, Let's say you are in the 15% tax bracket and are going to have $50,000 of taxable income this year. If you won't move up to the next tax bracket until you have $60,000 of taxable income, it may make sense to do a Roth conversion of $10,000.

This way you aren't pushed into a higher tax bracket and you get some money over to a Roth account in which it can grow tax free.

You will be taxed on any money that you convert to a Roth account so you will want to decide every year what the ideal amount is to convert.

Be Aggressive in Roth

If you are pretty familiar with the TSP, I am sure you know that there can be a significant difference between the performance of the G fund and the performance of the C fund.

The C fund is significantly more volatile but has the potential to grow much faster than the G fund. And in retirement it often makes sense to have some conservative investments and some aggressive investments so that you can provide for your short and long term needs. Because of this, some find it beneficial to put their aggressive investments in their Roth accounts and their more conservative investments in their traditional accounts.

For example, let's say you decide the ideal allocation for your retirement investments is 50% in conservative investments and 50% in aggressive investments. You could then put the more aggressive investments in your Roth accounts because whatever growth you get in that account will be tax free.

But again, you will want to be careful to not invest any money too aggressively if you are planning on spending it relatively soon.

Note: You will need a Roth IRA to use this strategy because you will need the ability to invest your traditional money and Roth money differently.

CHAPTER 8:

EVERYTHING ELSE

The TSP is an amazing benefit but I would be remiss if I didn't mention how your other benefits under FERS might come into play.

As an employee under the FERS, you will have income from three main sources:

1. **Federal Pension/Annuity**
2. **Social Security**
3. **Your TSP**

These are commonly called the 3 legs of your retirement stool.

When it comes to retirement planning, a great place to start is with your fixed income, AKA, your pension and social security. Once you have a ballpark on your monthly fixed income, you'll know how much you'll need from your TSP to cover everything else.

Federal Pension/Annuity

If you have some years before retirement, a good estimate of your pension is a great start. If you are eligible for an immediate annuity, you can estimate your pension with the following formula:

High 3 x Years of Creditable Service x Your Multiplier

Your multiplier will be 1% unless you retire at age 62 or older with at least 20 years of service, at which point your multiplier would be 1.1% (a 10% raise!).

For example, if you have 20 years of service, a high three of $100,000, and retire at age 63, your calculation would look like this:

$$\$100,000 \times 20 \times 1.1\% = \$22,000$$

This means that your gross pension would be $22,000 every year or about $1,833.33 every month. Your gross pension would then be decreased by any of your insurance premiums (FEHB, FEGLI, ect) and other things like taxes and your survivor annuity if you elect it. Make sure you do the math for your situation to know what your net pension will be. Your net pension is the amount that you'll actually get in your bank account after all the deductions.

Once you get about a year out of retirement, you should request a pension estimate from your agency to make sure their records match yours. It is not uncommon for them to make mistakes.

Note: If you are under special provisions (air traffic controllers, law enforcement, fire fighters) then your calculation will be different.

Social Security

The equation to calculate your social security benefits is very complex so the best thing to do is to go to ssa.gov and request a copy of your social security statement. On the top right hand corner of your statement will be an estimate of your monthly benefit at full retirement age. Your full retirement will be somewhere between 65-67 depending on your birth year.

The challenging part about social security is knowing when to turn it on. The earliest you can start benefits is 62 and the latest is 70. For every month you start your benefits before your full retirement age, your benefits will be decreased. However, for every month you wait to start your benefits after your full retirement age, your monthly benefit will be increased.

There is no cut and dry answer on when is the best time to to start but the things to consider are your life expectancy, financial needs, and your personal situation.

If you retire early, you may find it difficult to wait until your full retirement age to start your benefits. You will want to be careful to not deplete your TSP too much in the meantime. The best case scenario is to make these decisions long before you retire. This way you have plenty of time to know how you are going to handle every stage of retirement without stressing your finances.

Note: If you retire before age 62 with an immediate retirement, you will be eligible for the social security supplement or FERS supplement. While this benefit only lasts until age 62, it can help to bridge the gap between retirement time and when it makes sense to start social security.

Other benefits

While FEHB (your federal health insurance) and FEGLI (your federal life insurance) don't get as much attention as your other benefits, they all play a really important role during your career and retirement. Here are a few thoughts for each.

FEHB

I would argue that FEHB is one of your best benefits. Having access to great health plans while only paying about 28% of the premium (your agency picks up the rest) is incredible, especially as you retire and get older. You will want to make sure that you meet all of the eligibility requirements to keep these benefits into retirement. Some of the big ones are:

> ➢ You must have been enrolled in FEHB for the previous 5 years before retirement.

> ➢ You must be eligible for an immediate retirement.

FEGLI

Not everyone needs life insurance but it can be a deal breaker if you do. Some of the main reasons for life insurance might be so that your spouse/kids can maintain his/her standard of living if anything happens to you, or to pay off a mortgage or other debt. The first question you'll have to answer is if you need life insurance and if so, how much. Once you know how much you need you have to determine where to get it from. FEGLI does tend to get expensive as you get older, but it still might be the best option if your health might disqualify you from getting coverage on the private side.

FEGLI has similar eligibility rules as FEHB for keeping coverage into retirement, so make sure you fit the requirements if it is important for your plan.

CHAPTER 9:

THIS IS WAY MORE IMPORTANT THAN YOUR TSP

In my day job as a financial planner, I speak with a ton of feds within a couple years of retirement who are cramming money into their TSP as fast as they can. They are all trying to make up for lost time and do some last minute prep.

I have to admit though that in some areas of life, last minute cramming is my go-to method. Like taking tests in college. I knew that I would forget much of what I studied if I prepared too far in advance, so I often waited until the exam wasn't too far away.

The bad news though, is that the 11th hour cram doesn't work that great in retirement planning. To be honest, it actually doesn't work much at all. 11th hour retirement planning is less planning and more just finding out if you have to work longer than you want to. It becomes less about creating your dream retirement and more about accepting whatever benefits you can get.

And the worst part about last minute prep is not that your retirement benefits probably won't be as good as they could be but that you are leaving a huge portion of your life up to chance. Will you be able to afford your dream lifestyle and maybe that boat as well? Maybe. I don't know, but do you?

The best thing to do is to start now. Wherever you are at in your career. Start by thinking about what kind of retirement you want and then we can plan backwards from there.

Some people don't like the word retirement. This is often because they honestly don't know what they'd do if they didn't have work everyday. That is totally okay. At least for me, retirement is much less about not working and much more about **not having** to work. So for those that don't like the word retirement then we'll call it the day that work becomes optional.

But regardless of what we call it, think about what an ideal day looks like for you. What would you like to do or see? What would you like to not ever do again? Who would you like to spend your time with? Do you want to travel the world? Golf 6 days a week? Read for hours a day? Buy a beach house? For many of us it may be hard to describe the perfect day. That is okay. For some, the most important thing they want in retirement is the ability to do whatever they feel like in the moment.

These types of questions are the backbone of the retirement plan I build with my clients, and it should be a big part of yours as well. Because when it comes down to it, no one really cares about how much money they have in retirement or in life. What we actually care about is what kind of life we are able to live and create for our family. If we are able to enjoy a life that we absolutely love, then we don't really care about how much money we have in the bank.

Now, I am not saying that we shouldn't be prepared financially. All I am saying is that we prepare financially to create an incredible life. Not the other way around.

Once you have an idea of what you'd like your life to look like, then we can start finding the best strategies to get there. This is when we start looking at your TSP, pension, social security, and all your other benefits to maximize and optimize them for your goals. But these are just tools, and not the end goal. Even if I found the perfect TSP allocation and made 5 million dollars in the stock market, it would not matter at all if I wasn't happy at my job or in my relationships.

My hope with this book is that more feds will be a little better prepared for retirement. And maybe they will be a little more motivated to put more in their TSP. But I hope they don't do it for their TSP's sake. I hope they do it to create a life that they love. A life that excites them and that they are passionate about. A life that they just can't wait to get up every morning to live.

FINAL THOUGHTS:

I have spoken with federal employees all around the world and I am always impressed. In general, feds consistently work incredibly hard and are eager to learn. It is a great privilege for me to work one-on-one with federal employees to help them reach their goals.

After reading this book, if you have any further or follow up questions, feel free to reach out through my website at **https://hawsfederaladvisors.com/**.

Dallen Haws

MORE RESOURCES:

Our Podcast For Federal Employees

https://hawsfederaladvisors.com/podcast-page-2/

Our YouTube Channel For Federal Employees

https://www.youtube.com/channel/UCOVfyrVDS83jgo97HM0b
mNg/

Website and Blog For Federal Employees

https://hawsfederaladvisors.com/

29322042R00033